ROUND BY ROUND

First published in 2025 by Libri Publishing

Copyright © Bill Snaddon, Valerian Spicer and Andy Cole

The right of Bill Snaddon, Valerian Spicer and Andy Cole to be identified as the authors of this work has been asserted in accordance with the Copyright, Designs and Patents Act, 1988.

ISBN: 978-1-911451-39-6

All rights reserved. No part of this publication may be reproduced, stored in any retrieval system or transmitted in any form or by any means, electronic, mechanical, photocopying, recording or otherwise, without the prior written permission of the copyright holder for which application should be addressed in the first instance to the publishers. No liability shall be attached to the author, the copyright holder or the publishers for loss or damage of any nature suffered as a result of reliance on the reproduction of any of the contents of this publication or any errors or omissions in its contents.

A CIP catalogue record for this book is available from The British Library

Cover and Design by Carnegie Book Production

Libri Publishing
Brunel House
Volunteer Way
Faringdon
Oxfordshire
SN7 7YR

Tel: +44 (0)845 873 3837

www.libripublishing.co.uk

ROUND BY ROUND

Life Lessons from a Boxing Champion

Bill Snaddon with

Valerian Spicer and Andy Cole

FOREWORD

"I've known Valerian for a long time now, I remember being with her in Astana in 2016 for the Women's World Championships, and I've always been amazed by how far and how quickly she travelled in boxing from what was a late, standing start. It's an incredibly demanding sport but what's always impressed me most is that her story isn't a typical boxing story. Fighters very often end up fighters due to a lack of any other options. But Valerian had plenty of options and a comfortable life, however, to borrow a line from the book, she "resolved to fight her way into a life of meaning". I think that's a sentiment, an ambition, that will strike a chord with lots and lots of people. It's so easy to settle for something just because there's nothing really wrong with it, even though you know it's not what you want. It's human nature to be afraid to roll the dice, to put yourself out there to be shot at, or, in her case, punched, and I am sure that at times she was afraid but that didn't stop her doing it. She chose to step out of her comfort zone and force herself to get comfortable being uncomfortable. Valerian's my friend so of course I found reading her story enjoyable, but the real strength of the book is how relatable and accessible it is. The lessons in the text can be applied to all manner of scenarios and adapted to help overcome obstacles of all different shapes and sizes. I'm sure there were plenty of people who thought she was mad when she told them how she planned to quit her office chair for a corner stool but there was a method in her madness, A Spicer Method, and it's well worth studying! **"**

Andy Clarke, Sky Sports Lead Boxing Commentator

https://www.haughtonconsultancy.com/andy-clarke

CONTENTS

Foreword	v
Prologue	1
Round 1 *Listen to your dreams* Staying present – the S from the SPICER Method	9
Round 2 *Don't take your thoughts too seriously* Pivot – the P from the SPICER Method	25
Round 3 *Don't die with the music in you* Inner vision – the I from the Spicer Method	37
Round 4 *Find your middle ground* Centre yourself – the C from the SPICER Method	51
Round 5 *Breathing under fire* Exhale – the E from the SPICER Method	66
Round 6 *Plan, do, review, repeat* Routine – the R from the Spicer Method	75
Postscript – Breathing life into her legacy	87
The back page – Valerian's afterword	96
Testimonials	102

Valerian dedicates this story to her mum, dad, partner Laird and their children Hamish and Ceana

PROLOGUE

This is the story of a woman who at age 30 found herself in a rut and decided to dedicate herself to boxing. Within two years, she was an English champion. Within four years, she'd quit her office job and was flying around the world, competing at tournaments and beating some of the best boxers of the era. In her first international bout at the 2014 Commonwealth Games in Glasgow, Valerian, the underdog, defeated the world number eight. This win, like many in her career, would be against the odds.

In learning of Valerian's rise in the sport, it becomes clear that hers is not your typical boxing story. It's not the story of a troubled or misguided youngster from the wrong side of the tracks who's saved by the discipline and purpose that boxing offers. Rather, her story is that of an unfulfilled office worker who finds herself at a crossroads and chooses to walk down the path less travelled. Not wanting to die with the music in her, at age 30 she changes course and transforms herself into an elite athlete. The lesson to draw from her example, as psychologist Andy Cole sums up neatly at the end of each chapter is: if you have a dream and hold true to your vision, it doesn't matter who you are or where you begin. Whatever it may be, big or small, sporting or otherwise, you can make progress and turn your life around.

But let us rewind for a moment.

Valerian Spicer, the boxer – the sportswoman – had something to prove. Not to others, but to herself. As a young girl, she loved sport and was good at it. At 14, she was flicking through the TV channels and randomly stumbled across a documentary on ballet. Young Valerian was captivated by the athletic grit and toil required by these dancers if they were to reach the peak of their craft. While watching the documentary, she had a fleeting vision of the life she'd like to live. A life filled with purpose that was dedicated to the pursuit of excellence – committed to the idea of pushing herself to her physical limit while striving for a glimpse of perfection.

It was a noble ambition fuelled by lofty ideals. The trouble was, she didn't know what she wanted to do. And even if she did, she didn't know how to direct her focus. There was no ballast. The relentless drive she'd noticed within herself was scattered in various directions and her energy had nothing solid to grab hold of. Until, that is, she found boxing. Or, until boxing found her. It was then that she made the pivotal decision to throw herself into the sport. Along with her partner Laird, who would soon become her coach, they were all in.

When she pulled on the gloves, stepped through the ropes and onto the canvas, everything fell into place.

Valerian Spicer *(Credit: Raine McCormack)*

As her training reached new heights and her skills and confidence grew, that nagging feeling of drift that had settled in her stomach began to dissolve. As Valerian's potential was awakened, her restlessness – which had been morphing into resentment – began to evaporate.

Valerian was born in England to a British dad and a Dominican mum. Her dual English-Caribbean heritage, therefore, held open the possibility – if she was good enough – of representing Dominica on the world stage. When she began fighting competitively in gritty London boxing gyms, it wasn't long before her ability was recognised. At this stage, an international career came into view and, along with it, the option to pursue boxing for Dominica.

The idea, however, of representing the Caribbean nation on the world stage didn't always sit comfortably with her. She was worried about how it might be perceived in Dominica. After all, she hadn't been born there. This was playing on her mind. Understandably, having been born in England and spent her whole life in the UK, she felt much more British than Dominican. She was concerned that some people in Dominica might view her as an imposter – taking advantage of her mum's lineage in order to compete internationally.

As it turned out, her fears weren't completely unfounded. But on the flipside, any worries she had were soon overcome by love and support from the country. Family and friends in Dominica, and many strangers, embraced her decision. In turn, Valerian would more fully come to embrace this side of her heritage, which had been sitting dormant inside for her whole life.

Valerian acknowledges also that without the institutional backing of the Dominican Olympic Committee, none of this would have been possible. In particular, it was the general secretary of the committee, Thomas Dorsett, who made it happen.

When her career did get off the ground, not only did she have something to prove but she was in a rush. Entering the world of elite boxing in your early 30s (an age that would mark her as a veteran), of course she was in a hurry. There was a short window of time to prove she had what it takes at the top. A small amount of time to tap into that reservoir of potential she'd been aware of since she was little.

In November 2014, Valerian – the *veteran newcomer* to international boxing – fought at the World Championships in South Korea. It's no disgrace that she was eliminated from this tournament after losing to Katie Taylor, the Irish boxer who may go down as the best female fighter of all time. A few months later, she won a silver medal after boxing four times in five days at the International Boxing Association's Nations Cup in Serbia. In 2016, less than two years into her international career, she was named Dominican Sportswoman of the Year.

Owing to her humility, Valerian might have had trouble writing this book. Her understated nature might obscure the true extent of what she's achieved. That's

Valerian Spicer and Andy Cole *(Credit: Marcus Harvey)*

perhaps why I was asked to write it. I was approached to write the book by one of Valerian's friends, Andy Cole, after they had started their fitness and wellbeing programme called the Spicer Method – a combination of boxing training with the practice of mindfulness.

I had come to know Andy, a psychologist and metacognitive therapist, through my job at a UK health charity. Andy was working as a counsellor with some of the staff, myself included, using an approach called reflective practice, which allows people to process any emotional strain or trauma that might have been passed onto them as a consequence of their work. It's not uncommon in jobs where staff are exposed to serious illness or death. After the reflective practice sessions came to an end, Andy, who by this stage knew of my work as a journalist, mentioned that he and Valerian wanted to document Valerian's story and asked if I'd be interested in writing it.

After a few conversations we settled on a structure for the book. We decided to anchor each chapter to a story or moment in Valerian's career that brought to life a theme from her and Andy's Spicer Method. Spicer, of course, being Valerian's surname. And the Spicer Method can be explained as guide for leading a healthier and more balanced life, with each letter of her surname expanding into a wider theme, backed by psychological insights. S for 'staying present'. P for 'pivot'. I for 'inner vision'. And so on. These themes, supported by real-life lessons drawn from Valerian's career, can be applied by people at any stage of their life, no matter what your goals are or the situation you are in.

It made sense that each chapter would expand on a story that highlights the importance of each element of the method. For instance, in chapter one we see how Valerian, in her first international bout – a huge step in her career – was able to embrace her nerves, acknowledge the situation and enjoy the big moment. That is, she reaped the benefits of staying present.

At the end of each chapter, we hear directly from Andy, who offers a concise and practical summary for readers who might wish to apply some of Valerian's lessons in their own lives. These snapshots, coming from the mind of an experienced psychologist and imbued with digestible principles for better mental health, bring home the central messages found in each chapter.

The book draws on extensive interviews I did with Valerian and Andy, as well as others who have played a role in Valerian's story. Thank you, Valerian and Andy, for being so generous with your expertise and insights – and thanks to all those who gave time and effort in helping me along the way. Most of all, thank you, Valerian, for entrusting me to tell your story. Many hours of phone calls were had in the making of this book, with Valerian often juggling numerous commitments while tending to her two young kids, Hamish and Ceana. Her hope is that that when they grow up and read these pages, they will come to know their mum in a new light and be proud of what she achieved.

ROUND 1

STAYING PRESENT – THE S FROM THE SPICER METHOD

Listen to your dreams

Valerian steps through the ropes and into the ring. It's her first international fight, at age 34.

Opposite, across the canvas, stands a seasoned Olympic boxer. The noise from 10,000 people in the crowd washes through her. She notices the television cameras. Her ears catch the constant click and flash from photographers. Standing there with gloves secured tight, thinking back over how she got here, the improbability of it, Valerian looks up to her right and, by chance, amidst the flags and faces, sees her parents – her mum cheering wildly, her dad more composed. Both are waving to her. She gives them a wink. An involuntary smile emerges — a smile of a daughter who in that moment feels secure in her parents' pride. On this day in July 2014 at the Commonwealth Games, the biggest moment of her life, she's allowing the clamour and energy of the Glasgow stadium to narrow her focus. Nerves and doubt are also there, swirling around her stomach and mind.

Am I good enough? Do I belong here?

But she acknowledges the negative self-chatter without indulging it, without overplaying it. She embraces her anxious butterflies. Somehow, she's relaxed. She's not trying. She's being. The hard work has been done and it's time to enjoy the spotlight. It's time to fight.

Four years earlier, four years before this moment, it was a very different story. In 2010, then 30, Valerian Spicer found herself in a job and career she knew wasn't for her. She was miserable and felt stuck. Sitting in a London office, working as a business administrator for an executive search firm, she knew there had to be something else. More than that, there was a nagging feeling of ungratefulness. Because, all said, she had it pretty good. The question, though, known to many, was on repeat in her head.

What am I doing with my life?

She might also have been asking herself.

What has gone wrong?

She'd followed a path she thought was right – a conventional path. After attending a private girls' school in Suffolk on England's east coast, where she loved and excelled at sport, she went on to study criminology and law at university. This led into the office and a series of jobs that didn't sit right with her.

By 2008, she hadn't done any sport or proper exercise for almost a decade. Her passion for sport and competition had been suppressed and her unrealised potential remained just that. Unfit and sluggish in her late 20s, Valerian started kickboxing – the non-competitive kind without much contact. It was purely for fun and exercise two times a week. Soon, though, she got bored of this and, instead, joined a gym near her work. Again, just for fitness; no grand plans for international tournaments had yet entered her mind.

It didn't take long, however, before one of the instructors at the gym spotted rare talent in Valerian. He suggested she might think about competing in amateur boxing – seed planted. When Valerian told her boyfriend, Laird, that she was going to start boxing competitively, he burst out laughing.

"Really?" he said, as his laughter gave way to a look of mild concern.

Behind Laird's initial reaction, though, and underneath his self-acknowledged sexism, lay a belief in Valerian's ability.

It's worth noting the context here, made tangible by Laird's then-views on female boxing. His reaction to Valerian offers a window into the wider landscape of women's boxing, and women's sport in general. His thoughts on women's boxing were not uncommon at the time. Indeed, Valerian started boxing in 2010, a time when only men could box in the Olympics. Women boxed for the first time at the Olympics at the London Games in 2012, and for the first time at a Commonwealth Games in Glasgow in 2014. Further, when Valerian started boxing, many boxing gyms in the UK didn't allow women to join.

Returning to Laird's views, what really lay behind his worry was in actual fact a concern for the woman he loved. And truth be told, he wasn't convinced Valerian would be able to handle herself in the ring. In Laird's mind, and in many minds, boxing is not something to be toyed with.

In boxing circles there's a well-known phrase: *"You play football, rugby and cricket. But you don't play boxing."*

Having boxed himself and been around the sport for a long time, Laird's thoughts on this had some foundation.

And, understandably enough, he wasn't that keen on the idea of his life partner choosing a career that would see her getting punched in the face. Beyond all of this, though, Laird admits that when Valerian began boxing, he didn't think women should compete competitively. In his words: *"I didn't like the idea of women giving each other black eyes and emerging from the ring with blood all over them."*

Laird again: *"I realise now that I was wrong. It turned out that Valerian was more than capable of taking a punch, not to mention giving it back with interest."*

He also concedes that on the wider question of competitive female boxing, his concerns were unfounded. *"I have come to see that women, in many instances, are tougher than the men."*

From the moment they met nine years earlier, however, he had glimpsed her sporting talent. He remembers throwing her a set of keys to catch and she plucked

Valerian and Laird after winning her 2nd fight for Chadwell St Mary Boxing Club in 2011

them out of the air with one hand like a nonchalant baseball player. At this moment, with other memories also in his mind of her sporting abilities, he recalls thinking:

Bloody hell, this girl could be an Olympian.

Jump to 2010, after she'd been boxing at the gym for a while, she came home one day and was shadow boxing in the kitchen. Laird stopped, fell silent and thought:

Fucking hell, that's good!

He was convinced.

Laird himself had always loved sport and was a promising track and field athlete in his teens until a shocking ankle injury derailed his ambitions. As it happened, he was also obsessed with boxing, well versed in the craft and would train and fight as a competitive amateur boxer as best he could within the realms of what his body allowed.

He'd tried to get Valerian into boxing training years earlier, when he felt they both could do with the extra exercise, but the timing wasn't right, and she wasn't interested. Now, though, on her own terms, she was to get the bit between her teeth and go for it. Laird would be there for every weave, duck and punch.

Back in the Glasgow arena in 2014, Valerian, the 34-year-old newcomer to the stage, was battling it out against her more experienced opponent in the first two rounds. She thought she was on top but the scores

Valerian boxing in the English National Championships with her first boxing coaches, Chris Okoh, Scot Johnson and Steve Rogan

didn't show this. Her opponent, a tall, rangy fighter whose punches had reach, was the reigning New Zealand champion and had competed at the 2012 London Olympics. She had perhaps come into the contest thinking Valerian wouldn't offer much fight. Indeed, Laird had showed Valerian an article he found in the New Zealand press in the lead up which said as much.

"Look here Valerian," he said, *"the coach of this New Zealand girl thinks they've got an easy draw."*

He knew by showing Valerian the article it would fire her up and fuel her with added motivation. It would also play into Valerian's status as the underdog.

This was her first international fight representing Dominica, the tiny Caribbean nation where her mum was born and grew up. Valerian, born in England to a black Caribbean mum and a white English dad, holds dual British-Dominican nationality. The path to international boxing was down one of these roads, and it was the

Valerian training at Morrison's gym in Glasgow with her sparring partner DJ, and Dominica Coach McNeil Jules ahead of the Commonwealth Games, 2014

Valerian and the Dominica Team at the Commonwealth Games, Glasgow 2014

Dominican path that Valerian walked. This decision meant Valerian would be representing an island country with a population of 66,000 that few people have heard of. Whether she liked it or not, in the boxing world, she would be the underdog.

It should be said that New Zealand, on the world stage, isn't a big player, but in the Commonwealth Games it is. That is, in the context of the Commonwealth – the group of nations that once were territories of the British

Valerian Spicer's first International fight at The Commonwealth Games in Glasgow 2014

Empire – New Zealand holds much more sway than Dominica.

Sitting in her corner and getting her breath back, Valerian knows she's lost the first two rounds of the four-round bout. She can't hear him over the noise of the crowd, but Laird, sitting just off to the side of the ring, is shouting out to her, telling her to go on the attack. Her coach would deliver the same message in the one-minute break after the second round.

Valerian had two rounds left – four minutes of boxing – to turn things around. She needed a new approach.

Her natural mode as a boxer is more technical, focused on timing and footwork and being nimble and agile, commanding the centre of the ring by using skill and mind – while still being able to deliver powerful blows when the opportunity presents itself. In boxing parlance, this type of fighter is known simply as "a boxer".

Against this opponent, a more aggressive strategy was needed to take up the battle. She needed to apply more pressure. And though Valerian doesn't consider herself as this type of boxer – a "pressure fighter" – this is what she did. Put simply, she morphed from a Muhammad Ali into a Mike Tyson.

In the third round, her punches begin to land as her opponent stumbles across the ring. Valerian is in pursuit. The momentum shifts to the little-known Dominican fighter. The crowd sense what's happening, as do the commentators.

Valerian's mum, Helena, shouts uncontrollably from the crowd – *"Punch, punch, punch!"* – as she jumps from her seat.

Helena wasn't altogether pleased when her daughter told her she was getting into boxing. Understandably. How many mums want to see their daughter get punched in the face? She hadn't watched any of her previous fights. It was just too hard. But on this day in Glasgow, during her daughter's big moment, Helena lost herself in the moment as her Valerian took charge of the contest. Laird, too, was visibly happy.

"At this stage, the New Zealand boxer started unravelling at the seams," Laird recalls. "And Valerian is the nicest person you can ever meet, but when she gets the bit between her teeth, she's relentless. When she goes for it, she can punch really hard."

Down south in London, Valerian had more supporters cheering her on. Her sports therapist, Hazel Gale, who Valerian had been working with before the tournament, was watching the broadcast from her living room. Hazel recalls her own nerves in the lead up to the fight. Valerian, as well as a client, was also a friend. As Hazel is posting on Facebook in the minutes before the fight, drawing attention to Valerian's big moment, her hands sweaty in anticipation, her friend emerges on screen.

"I saw her walk out and I could just see it in her face, the moment she stepped out and the camera had her on. She was relaxed. She looked like she was there to have fun. She looked like she was there because she loved boxing." Her body language was that of a winner, says Hazel.

"When I saw her confident walk, I was screaming, 'Yes, yes, yes! Yes, Valerian yes!' Because for me, this was even more important than the boxing. Obviously, the boxing is important, but the body language, the walk, the sense of belief, had to be there. She had to have the right mindset *to get in there and box properly. And when she got in the ring and smiled at her family, she looked like she owned the place."*

The third round comes to an end. Valerian has turned the tide. The training, physical and mental, is paying off. The decision to change careers, from the office to the ring, is looking a good one. And in this fight, in the heat of the battle, her ability to change tactics – from her more natural tactical boxing to a more attacking style – has her on the edge of victory. Two minutes of hard work and focus stand before her and a remarkable win. She's the first woman boxer to represent Dominica at a major international tournament. She'll be the first female winner of a 60kg bout at the Commonwealth Games. (2014 was the first time the tournament had included women boxers and Valerian's fight was the first in the 60kg category.)

As the fourth round began, though, none of this was on her mind. She was executing her punches, one by one, remaining in control by pressuring her opponent with a relentless stream of attacks. She was not going to let her opponent back into the fight. If she did this, the rest would take care of itself.

The bell rings. The fighters bump gloves. They retreat for a few moments to their corners for a quick word with their coaches and a splash of water to the face. They return momentarily to the middle of the ring. The referee, now standing between them and holding both women at the top of the wrist, announces the winner after a pregnant pause by raising Valerian's arm. In those seconds, all exhaustion is gone. Delight takes over. Her face lightens from the focus that's held her together. The judges scored the bout very close but Valerian's strong finish secured the victory. She'd connected more punches. She looks up again to her parents and smiles beam back. A few Dominican flags are seen waving in the crowd, held by supporters celebrating their countrywoman's win.

And four years earlier, she had never boxed. Four years earlier, Valerian resolved to fight her way into a life of meaning. Leaving the stadium after that bout, she pops her headphones in and presses play on the song she was listening to on her way to the arena that morning. *Dreams* by Fleetwood Mac.

Valerian at the Commonwealth Games in Glasgow in 2014 after becoming the first 60kg boxer to compete and win her first fight. This was the first Commonwealth Games in history that women were allowed to compete in.

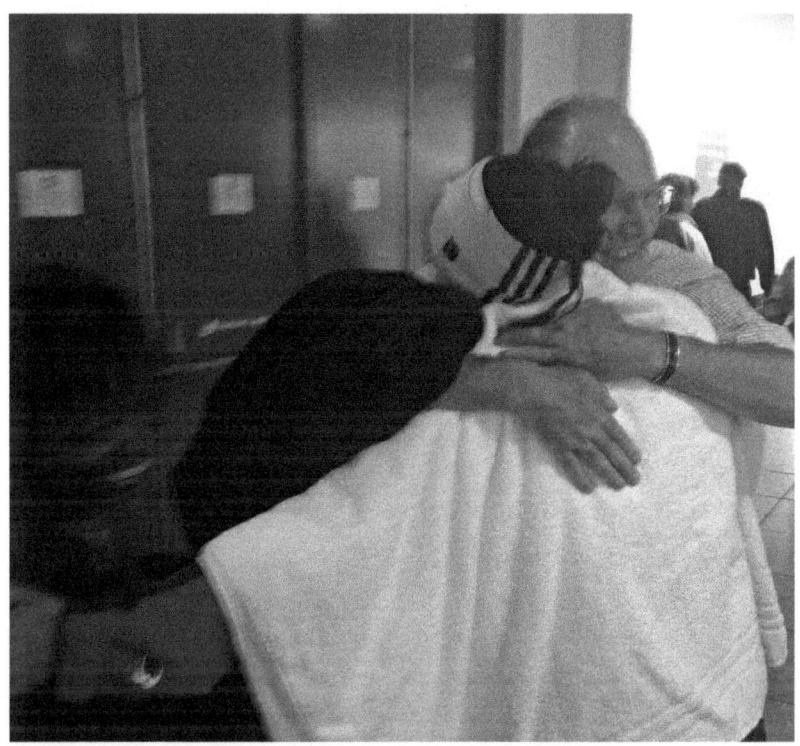

Valerian's mum and dad congratulating her after her win at the Commonwealth Games, Glasgow in 2014

ANDY'S TAKE ON STAYING PRESENT

There will always be things in our lives that we might start to worry about. We might often ask ourselves, *What if?*, on the basis that these types of questions seem to be helpful because they are about anticipating events and being prepared. The problem with worrying though is that is can lead to more worry, taking us further away from addressing the problems we are trying to deal with.

It is better to think of concerns, not worries. For example, why wouldn't Valerian have concerns about being ready for the fight? About turning things around after the second round? About representing Dominica? Importantly, concerns help us work out exactly what it is that we can do something about. They lead us to action, bring us back to the present and help us to accept our situation. Concerns help us recognise how we feel and help us decide what to do next. Addressing concerns leads us back to useful questions, like, *What can I do now?* or *How can I change this?* And if the answers to these questions are 'Nothing' or 'I can't' then you have uncovered some of your emotions – and can simply name how you feel. Emotions don't harm us. But how we think about them can.

Be present. Take action. Address concerns. Leave your worries on the canvas.

ROUND 2

PIVOT – THE P FROM THE SPICER METHOD

Don't take your thoughts too seriously

It's now February 2018, four years later. Valerian is entering the twilight of her boxing career. Many medals and trophies have been won since her international debut in Glasgow in 2014. But here, in this moment, she's got herself into a pickle. She's about to compete at a tournament in Sweden known as The Golden Girl. The event hosts a mix of domestic and international fighters and occupies a prominent spot on the calendar of European boxing.

Sitting in a hotel room in the city of Borås, near the western coast of Sweden, she can't shake the doubt and worry from her mind. Tomorrow, she's due to fight a rival, a seasoned international fighter who boxed for England, who two years earlier Valerian beat for the English Title Belt – a prestigious win in amateur boxing. After that victory in early 2016, Valerian heard on the grapevine that this opponent claimed she should have won and Valerian didn't deserve it. This led to an unbecoming Twitter spat between the two as their

Valerian at The Golden Girl Tournament in Sweden in 2018 12 weeks after giving birth

dispute played out in public view. Back then, Valerian remembers thinking:

How dare this boxer claim she should have won!

Needless to say, there was a sour feeling between the two boxers. As much as she tried, Valerian couldn't stop thinking about the Twitter spat and how her opponent had said she shouldn't have won. The looping memory was totally distracting her from the task at hand.

Valerian training with her sports therapist Hazel Gale at Islington Boxing Club

What if I lose tomorrow and then she'll say she should have won last time as well!?

Because she started boxing so late, at age 30, Valerian often felt like an imposter in the sport – that at any moment she might be found out for not being any good. Most boxers start much, much younger. This Twitter quarrel on the surface may have seemed innocuous, but it was feeding into Valerian's insecurities that she might not belong at the top of world boxing – even with a full trophy cabinet.

Valerian boxing in an Army dinner show pictured with her boxing coach, Bevis Allen at Islington Boxing Club

So, here she is, her mind stuck on something from two years ago, rather than focusing on how she can win tomorrow. On top of this, she hasn't boxed at a tournament since the middle of 2016. She's been out of the ring for a year and half since she retired when falling just short of making the 2016 Rio Olympics.

Back in the hotel room in Sweden, now 38, making a comeback, Valerian continues to question if she's made the right call.

Am I fit enough? Was this comeback a good idea?

Her concerns may well be warranted. Only 12 weeks earlier she had given birth. She and Laird, new parents, had come to this tournament in Sweden so Valerian could get some practice ahead of the Commonwealth Games in Australia later that year. Deep down, though, Valerian knew her fitness was nowhere near where it needed to be. She knew her timing, footwork and reactions would be off. She was not ring fit.

Am I crazy to go into a boxing ring 12 weeks after birth?

At times she thought she was. After all, every day in the lead up to that fight Valerian was expressing breast milk.

Valerian trained and sparred with her club mate, Nina Hughes, now former World Champion in the lead up to many of her fights

She had, however, worked her butt off to get here. She was lifting 100kg weights at six months pregnant, training up until one month before giving birth. And now, through hard work and discipline – *"a Spartan routine and eating like a bird"*, as Valerian put it – she'd dropped a remarkable amount of weight in the 12 weeks after birth, coming down from 85kg and now fighting at 64kg. Laird, who had given up a job in finance to become Valerian's full-time coach after the 2014 Commonwealth Games, was her drillmaster in this weight loss and get-in-shape campaign.

Before this bout in Sweden, Valerian was also carrying some guilt. Hamish, her 12-week-old baby, was back in England being looked after by Valerian's mum. She felt as if she'd abandoned her new-born to come to Sweden and fight. The niggling inner-chatter continued.

I'm a bad mum for being away from Hamish.

All of this was intensifying the rumination stemming from the Twitter dispute from two years earlier. She knew the dispute was petty but she couldn't wriggle it loose from her head. She knew she couldn't go into tomorrow's fight in this preoccupied emotional state. So, in that hotel room, she called her sports therapist and told her she needed help.

Hazel, I can't focus. I can't stop thinking about that Twitter spat and I'm fighting this girl tomorrow who thinks she should have won last time.

It might sound simple, and maybe it is, but Hazel asked Valerian to think of a song or something else she finds funny. What came to mind for Valerian was the theme song from the Benny Hill Show. This unmistakable tune, for Valerian, conjures up images of a comedian goofing around and a style of slapstick humour which appeals to

Valerian and Laird with Hamish training at the boxing gym

her. Immediately, her anxiety began to melt away. She found herself giggling.

Benny Hill, a well-known English comedian who had a longstanding TV show, popularised this tune by making it the soundtrack to the crescendo of his sketches as each programme closed. It's a fast-paced and light-hearted tune which, for those who recall the show, brings to mind burlesque-type comedy where Benny Hill, not the most attractive man, was often being chased around by half-dressed women. He, too, in a kind of creepy burlesque way, would often chase the women around. The comedy, of course, lies in the knowing absurdity of these scenes – we're all in on the joke. And even if you don't know the Benny Hill Show, this song – which actually predates the show and is known as Yakety Sax – is one of those songs that has the power to turn a grumpy frown into a reluctant smile; simply via the silliness or jovial nature of the sounds and melody it conveys.

Whenever she hears the Benny Hill song, Valerian gets the giggles. Beyond the hilarity she finds in the song, in that hotel room the tune also unlocked a carefree memory. Valerian remembered how at times she would playfully sneak up on Laird, in Benny Hill fashion, in a display, as she puts it, of her child-like sense of humour. This memory, linked to the song, also perhaps played a role in reducing the tension and anxiety she felt before the fight.

As a by-product of calling Hazel, she had stumbled across those precious commodities of perspective and humour – just when she needed to. The thoughts she was having about not being fit enough – these were now somehow refigured in her mind. She knew she wasn't fit enough but now, seemingly without trying, she accepted it – all because her mind was lighter and she wasn't putting undue pressure on herself.

In effect, the Benny Hill song meant her negative chatter had less of a grip on her. After all that, seemingly without trying and without effort, her mind now had the space it needed to pivot in a more positive direction. Her mind now had the space to think constructively about her fight. Valerian was now able to channel her anger and annoyance at this rival into something closer to focus. And, crucially, because she was now less anxious,

Valerian boxing a rival at The Golden Girl Tournament in Sweden in 2018

she wasn't over-thinking. Indeed, she felt less pressure *to* think.

The next day, as she walks from the changing room and into the ring, she's still humming the Benny Hill song to herself. She's still far from confident, but because she's now more relaxed, she has the awareness of mind to go into this fight and fake her confidence. That is, she can fake her confidence with confidence!

On the inside, she knows she's not ready, but she doesn't allow her opponent to see it. She steps into the ring, her body language strong and commanding. You'd never guess that 12 hours earlier her mind was a mess.

The fight begins. Valerian makes sure to dominate the centre of the ring, not allowing her opponent to set the tempo. She gets tired quickly but she doesn't show it. Exhaustion has set in but she maintains the power and output of her punches. The fake confidence, by osmosis, morphs into real confidence when she notices her opponent giving her too much respect. This encourages Valerian to punch harder. It offers fuel to her depleted tank. She finds energy to push on.

Twelve weeks after giving birth, having not competed at a tournament for a year a half, against a rival who had got her in head, Valerian finds a way to win. Then, something unexpected happens.

As her victorious arm is raised by the referee, the rush of winning joy she's felt so many times before doesn't emerge. In its place is something else. Something like relief, mingled with guilt. Her mind turns to her baby.

This win takes her into the final and she's happy about it, but more than anything, as a mum, all she wants is to get back to Hamish.

Looking back, she says: *"At the time, I didn't fully understand all the conflicting emotions I was feeling."*

Now, several years later, Valerian is coming to terms with the guilt she felt in those short stretches of time when she was away from her son. Her hope is that Hamish, when he's older, will see his mum's achievements in the boxing ring as an example of what can be done when hard work and determination combine in pursuit of a meaningful goal. The guilt she felt in those moments is now offset by her belief that Hamish will look to her legacy in the ring as a source of pride and inspiration.

On the comeback trail, after boxing three times in three days, Valerian went on to win a silver medal at The Golden Girl tournament. With all the chatter in her mind, knowing she wasn't in the best physical condition, she was able to pivot into a more optimistic and free state of mind. And she did it not by pretending the thoughts weren't there, but by seeking support and ultimately allowing the thoughts to be just that. She realised, at times, it's best not to take your thoughts too seriously.

ANDY'S TAKE ON PIVOT

Consider something that seemed important to you at one time but now you can't really remember much about. Imagine how many thoughts you had that simply came and went. When we start paying attention to our thoughts, those thoughts can proliferate and we start to dwell, wondering *What if* or *If only*, and it can get us too deep into figuring out why we feel angry, disappointed or tense.

Time moves on and we forget what we were thinking and feeling. But what if you were to discover that dwelling isn't helpful at all and that it isn't necessary to help us solve a problem. If you think less, you might well end up feeling better and more equipped – and you'll take less time doing it.

Valerian noticed how preoccupied she had become about her opponent. She started monitoring her emotions and actually began to feel worse. The song stopped her doing this. But it wasn't really because of the song. Natural distractions shift our attention, allowing us to dwell less and therefore we can be more present. And we don't have to do anything in order for this to happen.

Each of us has the innate capacity to recover from preoccupying thoughts without interference. Perhaps, after all, sometimes the best response is no response. Allow your attention to shift. Leave your thoughts alone.

ROUND 3

INNER VISION – THE I FROM THE SPICER METHOD

Don't die with the music in you

Valerian's mum sensed a restless drive in her daughter from a young age. *"She was always so busy, one thing to the next, so many things."*

Tennis. Hockey. Netball. Gymnastics. Karate. Juggling leadership roles at school with academic work. There was also modelling for well-known fashion houses and writing for the local newspaper. *"You don't talk Valerian out of something she wants to do,"* says mum Helena. *"That would be a waste of my energy."*

Valerian, too, recognised this drive in herself.

When she was 14, Valerian was flicking through the TV channels and stumbled across a documentary about the Bolshoi ballet school in Russia. After watching for a few moments, she put down the remote, captivated. She was glued to the screen for the remainder of the programme.

There was something about the Bolshoi, one of the world's oldest ballet companies, founded in Moscow in 1776, that spoke to young Valerian. The discipline

Valerian with her siblings Florna and Adrian as young children

and dedication of the aspiring dancers. The skill and technique that must be honed over arduous years of repetition and sweat. The raw grit required to make it through such a gruelling school that has produced some of the best ballet dancers the world has known. And, ultimately, the visual poetry that is achieved after painstaking practice pays off. The dancers bounding, floating and spinning – in seemingly effortless flow

– across the famed floorboards of the Bolshoi and other grand stages of the world.

This memory of watching that documentary and the feelings it stirred has stayed with Valerian. And it was with her throughout her whole boxing career, playing a particularly poignant role in her mind when was she was competing in countries that were once part of the Soviet Union.

Poignant because in those moments she realised, in her understated way, she had done something remarkable. Something not unlike those ballet dancers, albeit, of course, in a different discipline. Valerian was fighting on the world stage, boxing the best boxers in the world. She was at the top of her craft – and this was made possible only because she made some pivotal decisions and put the hard work in.

At the age of 30, she had given up a secure career that she had thought was right. For Valerian, though, the office job and corporate life was not meeting a deeper need. So, she took a risk and pursued boxing and was now living out a dream she'd unconsciously glimpsed while watching that documentary all those years earlier. At 14, she'd had a fleeting vision, not in the religious sense, but a vision of how she'd like to focus her energy in life. That idea of striving for excellence, in whatever field, had struck a chord with her and had stuck with her.

It wasn't the ballet, needless to say, that held appeal. Rather, what she sensed in that moment, and throughout much of her childhood, was that she wanted to direct her energy with purpose into something substantial. She didn't want to drift through life without pushing herself. In other words, she didn't want to die with the music in her.

"I was desperate to do something," she said. *"I just didn't know what it was."* Deep down, she knew it was something to do with sport but she had suppressed this thought once university began. Then life took over. But that nagging itch didn't disappear. Within her that drive was sitting idle, as if the gears had stalled. As her 20s rolled on, her stalled passion mutated into resentment and frustration. Her energy and talent had no outlet because her inner vision wasn't clear. Her energy had nothing to grasp hold of.

Then, at 30, she began boxing. Everything changed. Her mind became unstuck, creating space for a degree of clarity and direction to emerge. For Valerian, the very decision to start boxing allowed this new course to be set. No doubt the physical exertion from the training and the endorphins released created a healthy feedback loop, reinforcing the new vision emerging in her mind. The weaving and ducking and throwing of punches in the ring, the learning of new things, and the routine she now realised she'd been craving all along, all of this was washing away those nagging worries.

"All the feelings I'd been having while working in jobs that I knew weren't right for me. Knowing that it wasn't what I wanted to do with my career. All of that just disappeared when I took to boxing."

Valerian was grateful to those who employed her before her boxing career, and remains in touch with her last two bosses. One of them, Barney Kelham, became such a supporter of Valerian's boxing career that he made a last-minute dash to Glasgow to watch her winning international debut at the 2014 Glasgow Commonwealth Games.

For Valerian, the perennial questions of purpose and meaning – *What am I doing with my life and why?* – had for the most part vanished. The question disappeared because she had found an answer, or a response. Most important of all, she listened to that little voice in her head and chose to dedicate herself to this new pursuit. She loved the structure associated with boxing: her life was now anchored to something she believed in. With the wheels now in motion and her mind and body in sync, Valerian pulled off an incredible feat.

At 32, in 2013, having been boxing for only two years, she became the English national champion. In English boxing, in the 57kg category, there was no one better. Further evidence that her new direction in life – borne of the vision she now held to – was the one for her.

When asked about her drive and her ability to turn things around, and then adapt to change, Valerian thinks for a while before acknowledging the support of her partner (and coach) Laird. *"Without him, none of this would be possible,"* she says.

At the beginning, Laird admits to being sceptical of Valerian's decision to start boxing competitively. He also concedes that he once believed in the old school notion that boxing was only for men. This was not an uncommon belief. Once Valerian started boxing in earnest, however, he soon became her biggest supporter. He saw her talent, sure, and wanted her to fulfil her potential. More than that, he quickly came to see her dedication and love of the craft – and her willingness to take advice and her desire to improve. He saw this in most of the women Valerian was boxing against, too. A hunger to compete and win – equalling, if not surpassing in many cases, that of the men. Today, Laird is an unabashed supporter of female boxing.

Valerian ponders a little longer over this question of drive and her ability to adapt before mentioning her parents, who met in 1972 in Dominica – the island Caribbean home of her mum. Her dad, Keith, was on holiday from his job as a submarine cable engineer and was island hopping his way across the Caribbean Sea. Her mum Helena recalls the moment she met her husband-to-be.

"I was waiting for the bus on the 2nd of January, on my way home after spending the New Year's holiday with friends, and this white chap came up and said to me, 'Is the next bus going to Scott's Head?'"

It was. And Scott's Head, a small fishing village of blue ocean and gentle green hills on the southern tip of the island, happened to be where Helena's home was and where she was headed that day. In that moment when they met, Keith was on his way to the shops but he needed to get that bus, so Helena said she'd get the

Valerian's parents, Keith and Helena Spicer in the 1970s

driver to wait if the bus came while he was gone. Sure enough, the bus came and Helena got the driver to wait. Keith returned, jumped on the bus and sat next to Helena. They chatted the whole trip.

After his travels, Keith would journey back to England and from there would write a letter to Helena every week. Later that year, Keith returned to Dominica and stayed for a few weeks with Helena and her family.

The correspondence continued over the next year until, perhaps playing his trump card, Keith got his mother to write a letter to Helena. In that letter, Keith's mum, channelling Keith of course, asked Helena if she'd like to come to England and if so, she would have a place to stay with Keith and the family.

And so, in 1973, Helena packed her bags and headed for London, where she would begin training as a nurse, leaving behind her life and her teaching job in Dominica. Helena recalls the warm welcome from Keith's family in London as they helped her settle into her new life. On the day of her interview to become a nurse, she remembers fondly how Keith's dad took her to the interview on the bus and waited for her before both getting the bus back home afterwards.

Keith and Helena would soon get married and move east to Suffolk, where Keith's company had established a new headquarters. Before long, Valerian and her brother and sister would be in the world.

Valerian spoke about her parents in response to this question of drive and adapting to change because, in her parents, she had an example before her. Both of her parents had a clear vision of the lives they wanted to live and both were adept at dealing with change – and seeing challenges as opportunities for betterment and growth. In them, she glimpses something of what she saw in the Bolshoi ballet dancers: a desire to improve and build something through hard work.

In her parents, Valerian can see how open to experience they were and how they both took risks and threw a degree of healthy caution to the wind. Not reckless, but both followed a course in life that felt true to them. Her dad, who travelled the world with his work and also in his spare time, made lasting friendships with people all over the globe.

He would come home and regale Valerian with his stories of far-flung lands and the characters he had met, igniting a lasting curiosity for the world in his young daughter. And her mum, who set off for the UK in the belief that a more prosperous life lay ahead with a man she could see a future with. Helena's work ethic – toiling on long and constant nursing shifts – was not lost on young Valerian. Optimism, too, can be spotted in her mum when she recounts her childhood, growing up in 1960s Dominica.

Helena's family didn't have much money, but her mum and dad, through will and effort, made sure everyone was taken care of and that ends were met. *"We lived in a big wooden house and bred pigs and goats for eating. Before work, my father would take a little canoe out to catch fish using a pod made from bamboo. We had some land where we grew limes which my parents sold to a company who made drinks and jam from our produce."* All of this was done so the kids could get an education. *"There were many difficulties for the school fees each term,"* says Helena, *"but where there is a will there is way and my parents believed education was an investment in a productive future for us."*

After passing the entrance exam, Helena and her sister went on to attend the top girls' school in Dominica. She speaks fondly of her own mum as a devoted wife and mother, and it was her few acres of inherited land from where the family grew the limes to sell.

The strong social bonds of Caribbean life left a mark on young Helena, explaining how you enjoyed the moment you were in because tomorrow might not come. An appreciation for life in evident in her – alongside a belief that education is the path to a better future.

In her grandfather, too, Valerian had an example to draw on. He left school at 14 after his father died and began training as a carpenter to provide for his family. He became a skilled joiner and carpenter, building houses, boats and ornate furniture.

In 1955, then a young man, her grandfather was one of the 500,000 people from the Caribbean who moved to the UK in the aftermath of World War II. Britain was facing severe labour shortages. This group of immigrants who arrived between 1948 and 1970 became known as the Windrush Generation, named after the *Empire Windrush* – the ship carrying one of the first groups of West Indian migrants who arrived in search of jobs and a more secure future.

For two and a half years in the mid-1950s, Valerian's grandfather worked with a team of demolition workers, helping to bring down houses and buildings that had been damaged by Hitler's bombing raids on London. They were clearing the destruction and rubble so the new could be built. He would later work with his brother, who was leading a group of workers laying railway tracks en route out of London. All the while, both were sending money back to Dominica to support the family.

There are stories of note, too, on the other side of the family tree. After years of digging into the Spicer bloodline, Valerian's dad Keith unearthed a gem of a distant relative. He traced a familial link back to Grace Darling, the famed British heroine who risked her life one blustery night in September 1838 when rescuing the stranded survivors of the ill-fated *Forfarshire*. The paddle steamer struck trouble when it whacked against the rocky waters of the Farne Islands on England's north-eastern coast. It would have been just another shipwreck to drown in history if not for the lighthouse keeper's daughter. She, along with her father William, came to the rescue of the *Forfarshire*. Their heroics made front pages around the world. At home, Queen Victoria herself was suitably impressed, awarding daughter and father medals in honour of their bravery.

Closer to the present day but sticking with the ocean theme, Keith's dad, Leslie Spicer, was the principal engineer of the second largest tide-predictor machine ever built. Designed in the late 1940s, the Doodson-Légé machine had 42 pulley wheels that in conjunction with its other intricate components predicted the ebb and flow and the ocean's tide. The earlier model, the Roberts-Légé machine, was used by Britain and its Allies to calculate the timing of tides along the coast of northern France ahead of the Normandy landings on 6th June 1944. The ultimate goal of the landings, of course, was to get Allied troops and tanks onto European beaches. From there, they could launch the mother of all attacks to puncture Hitler's advances, driving the Germans back into Germany – liberating all those who had fallen under the Führer's yoke.

The humble tide-predicting machines were retired in the early 1960s as electronic computers took over the job. This story, though, tells Valerian that her dad (perhaps) picked up his engineering nous and interest from her grandfather Leslie.

Reflecting on these snippets of her history, Valerian now sees how those who came before her have had their own pragmatic plans for improving themselves. She can draw parallels between their mindsets and her own goal to realise her potential. In their ability to view challenges as opportunities for growth, she can see similarities in how she ultimately overcame her resistance and resolved to pursue a career truer to her own vision.

Watching that documentary as a 14-year-old helped unearth something inherent in her – something she shares with her mum and dad and grandparents on both sides, and many other relatives besides. That notion that our place in life is not fixed and it is within us to make the tweaks and changes that can set the course for a more fulfilling and productive tomorrow. Valerian was 30 when she grasped this; when she could more clearly see and acknowledge her vision. But the lesson it serves, she says, is universal and can be applied to any pursuit you deem worthy, big or small. And it's certainly not tied to a particular age or vocation or hobby. Rather, what she discovered was that when your mindset changes, along with your habits, a more meaningful life is possible.

The final thought on this chapter belongs to Valerian's dad, who died in 2017, when Valerian was five months pregnant and preparing for a comeback to international

Valerian and her dad after winning the English National Championships

boxing. When thinking about her idea to start boxing back in 2010, she recalls the unwavering support of her dad. She would have begun boxing, regardless, but with her dad's backing she felt the wind in her sails. He watched many of her bouts, cheering in his quiet way and telling his colleagues and friends about his daughter – the international boxer who was in the top 20 in the world. Her vision was given greater clarity and strength because of his encouragement.

ANDY'S TAKE ON INNER VISION

Inner vision is our ultimate *reason why*. It is often the thing that sustains progress once you have decided to get better at something – in sport, at work or in life. We feel more motivated when we are making progress against our goals and doing it alongside good people.

Valerian started boxing because she was talented and also because she made extra efforts to excel in her chosen field. She saw an opportunity to learn from everyone she encountered along the way, even if some of that learning felt really difficult at the time.

Having a vision about what we are trying to achieve will help us assess learning and performance over time. Choose something you like doing or know you are good at or would enjoy getting better at. Then, go and create as many opportunities as you can to experience doing it. The rest will take care of itself.

ROUND 4

CENTRE YOURSELF – THE C FROM THE SPICER METHOD

Find your middle ground

Valerian hasn't slept well. The adrenaline, mixed in with disappointment, is still coursing through her from the previous day's fight – a fight that didn't go to plan. She's in Bulgaria. It's October 2015. She's been knocked out of a tournament earlier than she would have liked.

She and Laird, who's now well-established as her coach, have a flight booked back to London but it's not for a few days. There's time, therefore, for Valerian to get some practice in with other boxers who, having been eliminated from competition, also have time on their hands before heading back to their home countries.

On the sidelines of major international tournaments, it's common when boxers are eliminated that they'll get some mutual practice in. It's a good way to make use of the unwanted time thrust upon them. As a compensation for losing, these opportunities offer a productive outlet to expand one's experience and skillset by sparring with opponents. It's a good way to hone footwork and sharpen punches and reflexes – all the while learning

Valerian training at an international training camp in France with the French and GB Team in 2015

about other boxers' strengths and weaknesses in the event of meeting them in future tournaments.

So, at 10 in the morning after her untimely defeat, Valerian and Laird turn up at the hall that has been converted into a sparring venue, not far from the arena where the tournament is held. A group of boxers are there, warming up, getting ready for training. Laird spots a boxer who he's keen for Valerian to go up against. He would often carry around a list of names of other fighters he wanted Valerian to spar with – and this boxer was in his sights.

On Laird's list were fighters who would help Valerian improve her own boxing. By getting her in the ring with

Valerian shared many rounds of sparring with double Olympic Gold medallist Kellie Harrington over her international career

a variety of top-class opponents, her repertoire of skills, and her confidence, would grow. It's much like how a tennis player, in order to keep getting better, needs to practice against a variety of opponents and on a range of surfaces. Bear in mind, too, that at this stage, in late 2015, Valerian is training intensely and competing at elite tournaments around the world with the goal of making the 2016 Rio Olympics.

As she begins sparring, though, she senses something isn't right. Valerian knew this boxer was good and had won some big tournaments, but hadn't expected this. The punches were coming at her much harder and faster than she had anticipated. She was holding her own and still commanding the middle of the ring, but on the inside, she was rattled. This rival of hers in the 60kg category had somehow got in her head.

"I lost my flow state and lost my clarity of mind," Valerian recalls. That effortless feeling that would often come to her in fights or sparring (which is not the same as not trying) was simply gone. She'd been knocked off her centre. Her internal compass that held her together in moments of physical or emotional stress had lost its bearing. Still, her body language wasn't revealing this internal hesitation to her opponent. But Laird, who knew Valerian's movements better than anyone, could see something was amiss.

Valerian and Laird at the Strandja Boxing Tournament in Bulgaria 2015

Valerian finishing sparring with her future opponent in Bulgaria

"Valerian was being a bit hesitant. It was a bit odd. I was wondering, What's the matter, why aren't you going for it more? If you were just a little bit more positive here, you'd really be getting the better of her."

Laird remembers the punches landing on Valerian's gloves with great force as she's blocking them away; he couldn't work out why she wasn't coming back at her harder. Perhaps, he thought, she's a bit tired from the recent travelling and the tournament fights. After all, they had been on a gruelling schedule for the past year. Or maybe, he thought, she could be overthinking – something Valerian herself concedes is the enemy of good boxing. In the ring, overthinking can get you into big trouble and takes you away from your composed and relaxed middle ground – the place where you want to be. That is, overthinking can lead you to being dangerously distracted.

"It can start with your thoughts," she says. *"If negative thoughts are coming into your head and you lose control of these thoughts, then your emotions can get the better of you. This manifests into the physical and you then have much greater difficulty in executing what you need to do."*

Rather, you want to be in that state of flow where your training and experience take over. Ideally, you want to be acting and reacting on intuition, instinct and skill. When this happens, enjoyment can kick in – even if your opponent is trying to punch you in the face

You still want to be thinking, sure, but you want that thinking to be nimble and fluid – as if your mind is at one with your body, says Valerian. It's when that thinking drifts into second-guessing yourself – or wondering too much about what your opponent might be up to – that things can get messy. When your thinking takes you away from your task at hand or distracts your focus, you need to gently catch it and acknowledge it, without getting down on yourself. This mere act of observing your thoughts without judgement can help shift your state of mind back to a more composed centre.

Back on the canvas, Valerian is on the receiving end of a stinging backhand. This was her cue, a painful one, to gather herself. She knew she had to make the best of these training opportunities against her peers and so she accepted her situation. Going through her mind is:

These punches are coming in and it feels like I'm a step behind but I know I will get through this and make the most of the spar.

These spars were also ideal opportunities for her to put into practice the psychological elements of the sport she'd been working on outside the ring.

Around this time, Valerian had been working with her sports therapist on visualisations that would help sharpen her technique. In this spar, as the punches were flying, she began to tinker with one of these visualisations. It was aimed at getting her to quickly lift up her back foot, which would occasionally drag for too long on the canvas as she executed a backhand punch. You want your back foot to pick up off the ground as you follow through on the punch, giving you more oomph and momentum. If you get the timing right and you're the right distance from your opponent, you're more likely to connect a flush punch.

In the ring here, Valerian was visualising a lightning bolt hitting the back of her heel as she punched, making her instinctively lift up her foot – the same sort of thing as imagining the back of your heel has just touched hot coals.

Focusing on this micro-component of her boxing helped take her mind from the power of the punches coming at her. But, while she got some good practice in and got through the session without outwardly showing too much concern, Valerian stepped down from the ring with some lingering doubts.

In the locker rooms afterwards, looking in the mirror, she admitted to herself that her confidence had taken a hit. This is something she would talk about with her sports therapist, but no one else. Allowing signs of weakness to be seen or rumours of lost confidence to be let loose is not something you want in the boxing world. It's a part of the sport that both Valerian and Laird talk about. By its nature, boxing can be brutally tough and ruthless, but running alongside this can also be great vulnerability. Indeed, in the ring, if you're not physically or mentally prepared you're opening yourself up to danger.

And so, to shake off the doubt, Valerian doubles down on her training. She gets back to her routine and throws herself into the structure that has served her well. The familiarity of this practice – *come back to the routine, come back to the routine* – offers respite against the doubts that had crept in. It's as if this structure and routine give her antibodies to fight off those pesky little negative voices that we all hear.

She's now in the top 20 in the world and knows she's better than that performance at the training gym in Bulgaria. Before long, her confidence returns and that memory fades. Then, as it happens, three months later,

Valerian boxed 4 times in 5 days to win a silver medal at the Nations Cup Tournament in Serbia in 2015

Valerian is drawn to fight this same opponent at a tournament in Serbia.

January 2016. All the top boxers are in full swing trying to qualify for the Rio Olympics, six months later. This tournament, The Nations Cup, held that year in the northern Serbian town of Ruma, hosts boxers from round the world. Top-shelf talent is on display, with countries each year sending their best fighter to compete.

Valerian boxing a rival in the Nations Cup Tournament in Serbia in 2016

When Valerian finds out who her next opponent is, the memory from three months earlier floods back in. She recalls the power of those punches and the feeling of being one step behind. Importantly, though, she chooses not to dwell on this memory. She doesn't allow the memory to run away into doubt and worry. She acknowledges it, while reminding herself she's done everything possible in the past three months to strengthen her game. Despite their past encounter, she allows herself to go into this fight with confidence – even if some of that confidence is faked.

Plus, Valerian has done her homework on this opponent. She knew this fighter was a strategic type of boxer who would try to control the centre of the ring – not dissimilar from herself. She also knew this boxer had a strong hook, left and right. This intel informed Valerian's strategy, the knowledge armed her with power.

For Valerian to control the tempo of the bout, therefore, and dominate that all-important middle ground, she resolved to use a lot of feints throughout the whole fight.

The plan with these feints was to draw her opponent in and induce from her an ill-timed attack. Valerian was luring her with a trap to create opportunities in space and time for her own counter attack. And, Valerian now noticed her timing was spot on, meaning her opponent was constantly on the back foot. Valerian's "distance" too, was also well judged. That is, she was in range when she wanted to land a punch and was out of range when her opponent was trying to hit her.

All of these tactics combined were keeping Valerian's opponent second guessing, limiting opportunities for her to wield those powerful hooks. Valerian was blunting and diffusing her opponent's strengths.

If carried out well, this particular type of feint – of pretending to throw a punch and then pulling back or signalling you're about to throw a punch to the body but then at the last moment throw a quick jab to the head – can prove remarkably effective.

As the fight goes on, Valerian's confidence grows. It's exhausting, constantly feinting and biding your time before you deliver a blow, but the strategy is paying off. What's more, she remembers thinking:

Hmm, she doesn't punch as hard as I thought she did.

This infuses her with courage. They enter the final round. Valerian holds strong and finishes off the fight as she began: in control, dictating terms.

The scorecard reveals a close fight. Valerian emerges victorious. Best of all, thanks to her deft feinting and attacking posture, she doesn't recall receiving a direct punch the entire fight. Again, here, some fake confidence grew into real confidence. Many faked punches, with a few solid connections in between, led to a well-crafted win. She'd also put that lightning bolt visualisation into practice with her back heel now jolting up when launching forward with a backhand offensive.

Happiness and a tinge of relief sets in as her tired legs step down from the ring after the fight, on her way to a semi-final and bronze medal at the tournament.

Valerian would face this opponent one more time in her career in what became a bizarre encounter – an encounter that would likely come to explain why those

Valerian at the international training camp in Kharkov, Ukraine 2016

punches from their first spar back in October 2015 had felt so powerful.

This time, they met at an international training camp in Ukraine in April 2016, a few months after Valerian's Nations Cup victory. They'd been sparring for a few rounds at this Ukraine camp before Laird noticed some foam-like material sprinkled across the canvas. He stopped the session and asked to take a look at her gloves. It became clear then that the foam was leaking from the opponent's gloves. Laird spoke to the opposing coach, requesting that his charge remove her patchy, thin gloves and put on a pair with the necessary padding – as the laws of boxing require.

This might explain the smack coming from her (foamless) gloves – and, this is probably what had happened back at that Bulgaria spar in October 2015, when Valerian, now with some vindication, said it was like getting punched by a bare fist.

Why would a boxer do this? For any number of reasons. But it's likely done to give them an unfair – not to mention dishonest – edge over an opponent in training, hoping that that psychological advantage will carry over if they are to meet in an actual fight. What Valerian showed is that training hard and sticking to her routine, while keeping a strong mindset, ultimately proved a more powerful approach. Under pressure and under attack, she was able to find her middle ground and win.

ANDY'S TAKE ON CENTRE YOURSELF

We often feel troubled, cautious or fearful about what's coming next. This can trigger negative thoughts or feelings which are familiar, believable and sometimes just how we think things are.

But what if you were to discover that, by spending less time on the things you usually ruminate or worry about, you would think less badly about yourself and feel much better more of the time?

To centre yourself is to switch your focus to the here and now. By paying attention in a different way, we can become less preoccupied by events in our minds and don't have to spend mental effort figuring out why things happened or anticipating what will happen next.

The only thing that we can influence is what's happening right here, right now. Valerian used mental techniques to refocus her attention away from the things she was becoming preoccupied by, away from the things she knew did not help her. When she returned to the here and now – centring herself – she found her confidence returned.

ROUND 5

EXHALE – THE E FROM THE SPICER METHOD

Breathing under fire

Valerian doesn't think of herself as one who stands up to bullies. The evidence, however, points in the other direction. When she was 16, toward the end of secondary school, she heard that a group of younger students were being pushed around and taunted by another girl. Not having any of this, Valerian intervened and had a polite yet robust word with the bully. The girls had no trouble from then on. To show Valerian their appreciation they wrote her a card.

Twenty-five years later, Valerian's mum Helena came across this card while she was sorting through some old files. Helena recalls the moment she happened across this now-family-heirloom.

"When Valerian left for university, my husband Keith wanted to re-purpose her room into a space where he could indulge his love for gadgets and technology. Keith was a real radio ham. When converting Valerian's room into his radio shack, we came across some of Valerian's school documents and began boxing them up for safe keeping. Filing some of her school projects into a box one morning, I came across a

card that was from 11 girls from her school. It says: "Dear Valerian, thank you for getting rid of Sarah. Lots of love, everyone!" I found out later that Sarah was the school bully. And all of these children were grateful to my Valerian, with their signatures at the bottom of the card! They even drew a photo of a hockey player on the front of the card because Valerian was captain of the hockey team. I said to Keith that we had better keep this one safe."

Valerian has little recollection of this incident and plays down its significance when asked about it. Perhaps, she says, as deputy head girl of the school and hockey captain she was doing what anyone with her responsibilities would do when they see an injustice.

In 2015, in a case of history repeating itself, Valerian found herself standing up to another bully.

Now 34 and one year into her international boxing career, she was at a hastily arranged two-week training camp in Florida. Compared to her recollections of dealing with the schoolyard bully Sarah all those years earlier, her memories of dealing with this more recent bully are clearer.

It was mid-September. She and Laird had travelled to America to visit Valerian's sister Florna, who lives in Florida and had been unwell. Normally, Valerian's dad would travel there once or twice a year to visit Florna, but he'd had a stroke a few months earlier and was still recovering.

At this stage, Valerian was training flat out in her campaign to make the 2016 Rio Olympics. Laird,

Valerian with Bonnie Canino and Yvonne Reis at Canino's Boxing Gym in Florida in 2015

therefore, had arranged some sparring at a local gym to ensure her preparation remained on track.

Drawing on his knowledge of the international boxing world, Laird contacted Bonnie Canino, a pioneering figure in women's boxing. Bonnie would then go onto to arrange some sparring at her gym for Valerian.

During her heyday, Canino won world titles in both boxing and kickboxing. In the 1980s and 90s, along with other trailblazing female fighters, she also stared down the stubborn sexism in the sport, knocking down prejudices and opponents and paving the way for Valerian and other boxers who emerged a generation later.

Outdated views on gender still persist in boxing, but the efforts of Canino and the example set by her class of boxers smoothed the way for the current crop of fighters. Increasingly, today, gender isn't a question. Rather, in the ring, the gender-blind notions of hard work and determination trump the stereotyped ideas of manliness and femininity and all the baggage these words dredge along.

Back in Florida, it was a hot and humid Tuesday morning. Canino greeted Laird and Valerian outside the gym in Dania Beach, just north of Miami.

Canino, a local, is used to the heavy, muggy air. But for Laird and Valerian, the humidity is palpable in every breath. For Valerian, this starts to play on her mind as she walks into the gym, wondering if she'll be able to get enough oxygen into her lungs during the sparring.

As she's stretching and warming up, taking note of Canino's trove of trophies and medals displayed around the gym, her sparring partner walks through the door, late. She strides in with that unmistakable American swagger, full of confidence and more than a hint of arrogance. Bravado might get close to the mark.

She walks past Valerian, brushing her eyes up and down over her British visitor, attempting to intimidate. Valerian, her Britishness coming through, attempts a courteous hello. Her opponent ignores her. No words are exchanged before they jump into the ring, which isn't uncommon before two boxers who don't know each other are about to spar. Still, Valerian thinks this boxer is trying a bit too hard and laying it on a tad thick, considering this isn't a tournament or club bout.

As the two women are putting on their gloves and shaking off any pre-spar jitters, Bonnie approaches Laird to say the other coach wants this spar to be four rounds of three minutes each. At that time, elite Olympic female boxing was four rounds of two minutes. This tweak to the timing was sprung on Laird and Valerian.

As the humidity cloaks and chokes the gym, Valerian and her sparring partner step forward to spar. Valerian comes out of the blocks fast and aggressive.

"She didn't shake hands or touch my gloves beforehand," says Valerian, *"you always touch gloves to start off. She clearly wanted blood – she was coming out to kill me. And that ignited something in me, and I was like, 'Well, she isn't going to get the better of me, ever.'"*

What happened next has stayed with Valerian.

"I remember getting loads of punches in. I felt like I was trying to punish her. She came at me and I then got on top. I got good shots in but she was still coming. I was throwing everything at her and she just kept coming. It was like this for most of the spar. We found ourselves at close range working on the inside, toe to toe, hooks to the body, upper cuts to the head, then, out of the blue, she calls me a bitch.

In my head I was like:

What?! This has never happened before, what's going on?

It just made me want to punch her even harder."

Valerian came back to the corner after that round, took a seat and some deep breaths to catch enough oxygen through the thick air.

Laird saw that something wasn't right.

"What's the matter, you're looking pensive?"

"I'll tell you later," says Valerian.

"No, tell me now."

"She just called me a bitch!"

"Well, what are you going to do about it?"

Valerian didn't require further encouragement. Despite the heavy conditions and the underhanded approach of her opponent, or perhaps because of it, Valerian came out after that break and took the bull by the horns. But it wasn't anger she was feeling. Any anger she might have felt morphed into focused aggression and a belief that she would get the better of this mouthy upstart.

Without really thinking, she's channelling her indignation into letting her shots fly and land on target, exhaling rhythmically on the extensions of each punch. Fuelling her further, in a harmonious and satisfying feedback loop, was the sound of the smack of her gloves against her opponent's face and body. Valerian was in a state of flow.

"Valerian gave her a pasting," said Laird. *"She wasn't thinking about technique at this point, she was on autopilot."*

As Valerian grows throughout the spar, her opponent, whose coach wanted the longer rounds, begins to tire and falls away. Valerian's fitness and grit came to the fore.

After the session, the other boxer and her coach packed up their gear, shoulders slumped, and headed out of the door into Florida's midday heat. Again, no pleasantries were exchanged. This time, though, Valerian wasn't too upset.

What Valerian drew from this encounter was the importance of channelling her emotions into a productive response. That is: don't get angry, stay focused and beat the crap out of your opponent. Or, rewinding for a moment, if we go back to how she dealt with Sarah the schoolyard bully from all those years earlier – she stayed calm yet in control and stood up to an aggressor, paving the way for a friendlier environment at her school.

She also took confidence from this Florida spar, knowing she was able to overcome the tough conditions. And it was her breathing, in no small part, which helped her to do it. She had learnt from earlier in her career not to panic in such a humid or tense environment, and to accept the conditions as they are. Here, in Florida, she was consciously aware of her breathing and the importance of her exhale as she executed her punches. She was aware of the need to take long, deep breaths in between the rounds. The focus on her breathing, above all else, kept her grounded when the vicious punches and verbal abuse were coming at her.

Two days later, Valerian was scheduled to spar the same boxer again at Bonnie's gym. The opponent didn't show.

ANDY'S TAKE ON EXHALE

Breathing is at the heart of any mindfulness approach and works without you having to do anything other than switch attention to your breath.

Valerian upped her tempo and increased her power by focusing on her breath. Breathing prepares us, sustains us and helps us recover. Power is replenished, calm is restored and we remain more in the moment.

Observe your breathing right now. What do you notice? Is it cooler as you breathe in? Warmer as you breathe out? Imagine you can follow your breath as it enters your lungs. Can you feel it working? Relax into your breathing and stay awhile, breathing gently, deeply and fully. You just did a mindfulness exercise. Not so difficult, is it?

ROUND 6

ROUTINE – THE R FROM THE SPICER METHOD

Plan, do, review, repeat

Valerian lost 28 kilograms (61 pounds) in the four months after having her first child so she could get back in the ring to compete at the 2018 Commonwealth Games in Australia. Asked how she did this, she said one word: routine.

As mentioned in an earlier chapter she elaborated on this, somewhat in jest, by adding: *"A Spartan routine and eating like a bird."*

Now, looking back over her career, Valerian can see how in many bouts she gritted her way to victory thanks to her preparation. It was thanks to a routine and the rigorous training she'd put in long before the fight that meant, more often than not, she came away with the win.

Or, as Muhammed Ali put it:

"The fight is won or lost far away from witnesses – behind the lines, in the gym, and out there on the road, long before I dance under those lights."

And so it was for Valerian in May 2016 at the World Championships, in the central Asian country of Kazakhstan. This tournament, while being prestigious in its own right, was also the final opportunity for these boxers to automatically qualify for the Olympics later that year in Brazil. The World Championships is a big event in any year but particularly so during an Olympic year where boxers are vying to move up the rankings to secure a prized spot in the Olympic draw.

Much was at stake for this crop of top-flight boxers as they arrived in Astana, as the Kazakh capital was then called. The atmosphere was tense.

But for Valerian, when the plane touched down, she was aware that her mind wasn't in it. The nervous energy she was used to feeling before a tournament had all but vanished. It was disconcerting. Laird, as well, was concerned. He knew her better than anyone and could see she wasn't focusing as she had been for the past couple of years.

Around this time, too, Valerian recalls that her body had begun to feel the strain.

"I had been working so hard, it had been non-stop — the training and preparations. I'd squeezed in so much since I started boxing internationally in 2014. Training and travelling and competing had become my full-time job. So much physically and mentally had been put into boxing up till this point — maybe my body was failing because I'd been pushing too hard. It's interesting that it all seemed to happen at exactly that point when I mentally dipped. I went

off form. I hadn't completely deteriorated but I wasn't on form like I had been. I was 36 by this stage. I think it was the mental drop-off that manifested in the physical decline. I don't think it was just coincidence that the mental and physical concerns all happened at the same time."

She traces the beginnings of this feeling of decline to a tournament a few months before the World Championships. Valerian and Laird were in the Argentinian capital of Buenos Aires in March 2016 for an Olympic Qualifying tournament for boxers from the Americas. Representing Dominica, where her mum was born, Valerian's campaign to make the Olympics was on track. She was aiming to be the first Dominican, male or female, to box at the Olympics for the Caribbean island nation. According to those in her corner, she was at the peak of her powers. Many observers at the time noted the quality of her boxing.

By several accounts, during this run of form in late 2015 and early 2016 she should have scored a victory against the soon-to-be Olympic gold medallist. The three judges scored the bout a draw, meaning the final call rested with one judge. This deciding judge gave the win to Valerian's opponent.

Laird remembers losing his cool when the decision was announced, loudly letting slip a string of strong adjectives from the corner on hearing Valerian hadn't won. He was infuriated with what he perceived as a wrong decision – an injustice, even. But in the subjective world of boxing, where humans are scoring, questionable judgements are not uncommon.

Valerian winning a bronze medal at the America's Continental Championship in Bolivia 2016, she was the first boxer to win a medal at a Continental Championship in Dominican history.

Valerian and Laird at the Americas Continental Championship in Bolivia in 2016

Even the modest Valerian allows a moment of pride when remembering how she was boxing in the lead up to Argentina.

"I was on fire up until Buenos Aires."

Coming into the tournament, she had put the previous questionable decision out of her head – and by the time she got to Argentina her mind and body were in sync. Her Olympic dream, too, was still very much alive.

When asked how she got her mind into a better place after a setback or a loss, or a decision she didn't agree with, she says:

"You just get back in the gym straight away and you get back to your routines, that's how your mind rejuvenates and how your body prepares for the next fight or tournament. If you don't have the routines your mind just goes wild – your thought process can go all over the place."

Valerian had cruised through to the quarter finals in Argentina and was now up against a trailblazing Latin American boxer who was well known in the region – most notably for being the first female to win gold at the Pan American Games when this tournament opened its ranks to women in 2011.

Then, in what felt like a re-run of many prior bouts, Valerian and Laird thought she had the win but the decision went against her. This loss was the straw that broke the camel's back. It took the wind out of her sails – not only because she sensed the judges had got it wrong but because the Olympics were now all but out of reach. She needed to have progressed a few more rounds in this tournament to gain the necessary qualifying points if she was to make the Olympics. Valerian remembers it clearly.

"I felt a mental decline with everything that happened after Argentina. I knew that it would now be extremely difficult to make the Olympics and my career might soon be coming to an end."

With the scene set, we now return to the World Championships in Kazakhstan in May 2016. She's got niggling injuries all over her body and the loss in Argentina two months earlier had precipitated a dip in her competitive spirit. On top of it all, her dad's

Valerian qualified to box in the Pan American Games in 2015

health had recently taken a turn for the worse when his prostate cancer was deemed terminal. He would live one more year.

On hearing news of the diagnosis, she wiped the tears from her eyes. Boxing all of a sudden didn't seem so important. But she wanted to do her dad proud at this tournament. He was her biggest fan. He'd supported her step into boxing from the beginning. He'd watched his daughter go from never boxing before at age 30 to becoming an English champion at 32, then to becoming a top-20 world boxer a few years later. He followed her rise as she competed all over the globe against the best boxers of the era.

The bell rang to signal the start of her first bout in Kazakhstan. Valerian whacked her gloves together and walked toward her opponent, an up-and-coming Hungarian who had recently won a medal at the World Youth Championships.

The first round was messy. Neither boxer got any clean shots.

In her corner, Laird was thinking, *What the hell is Valerian doing?*

The answer to this question is that all of her concerns and worries had been brought into the bout. She couldn't focus. Then, toward the end of the second round, Valerian instinctively shifted to another gear. All her thoughts and worries hadn't disappeared but she'd now found a higher level where these concerns weren't obscuring her focus.

Valerian boxing at The World Championships in Astana, Kazakhstan in 2016.

Experience and skill, borne of training and competition, had taken over. The fruits of her routine were now being seen.

She connected some wonderfully flush punches, one of which was beautifully captured by a ringside cameraman. The accumulation of these clean punches led to the fight being stopped. Valerian was declared victorious by a technical knockout.

Despite the mental dip and fatigue she'd felt before the tournament, her experience proved the vital ingredient in overcoming the younger opponent.

She will say afterwards that this win, more than anything else, can be put down to one thing. Routine. It was the effort, often repetitive, sometimes boring, but the effort over many years that got her over the line.

This win sticks in her mind because it showed her what can be done when you're not feeling your best. It offers her proof that what you're feeling inside doesn't have to be what you present to the world. In other words, you are not your thoughts.

In the next round of the World Championships, Valerian would lose to a Russian boxer and was knocked out of the tournament. She got the news shortly after that she'd just fallen short of making the Olympics. It was devastating. With time, she has reframed her disappointment into something more positive – focusing instead on the things she's achieved in boxing. With time, Valerian has viewed her career with more perspective and given herself due credit for the success she achieved in such a short time after coming to the sport so late. Not many have done what she did.

As the plane leaves Kazakhstan in late May 2016, she decides it's time to retire. In retrospect, however, she concedes that this was only ever going to be a temporary break from the sport, giving her mind time to reflect and rejuvenate. She always had half an eye on making a comeback for the Commonwealth Games in Australia in 2018. But for now, she and Laird had been planning to start a family – and this was the time.

A new routine would soon begin, building on what she'd learnt so far throughout her life and boxing career. A comeback indeed was around the corner, followed this time by a proper retirement. At age 38, Valerian would then find herself at a crossroads. Would she go back into the office and pick up where she left off before boxing? Or would she lean into her passion and pass onto others what she had learned during a remarkable sporting career?

You may have guessed that she chose to stay involved in boxing. And this has been to the benefit of many others. Valerian has gone on to become a trainer and coach, introducing people of all levels to the joy, challenge and rewards of boxing.

Running through all her work, her guiding philosophy, is the role of routines. In whatever sport or pursuit it is, big or small, Valerian emphasises the importance of developing a routine that works for you. Routines kept her on track, kept distractions to a minimum and allowed her to focus on what really mattered.

ANDY'S TAKE ON ROUTINE

What would you like to get better at? How much do you know already? Maybe you have the know-how but need skills practice? Or do you need to find opportunities to gain more experience and apply those skills?

Think of it like this. Knowledge – Know-How – Show-How – Expertise. Valerian's expertise won through in tough times because she had the *know-how* and could *show-how*. And a large part of that is having a routine. In sport, in work or in life we will make significant gains when we *plan, do, review, repeat*.

If we stick to a routine, we will become more practised, gain more skills and apply these in new and different ways. Sometimes we might think we're not moving forward, even though we are. That's normal. Don't be disappointed. Stay with it.

POSTSCRIPT – BREATHING LIFE INTO HER LEGACY

Let us rewind to November 2017. Valerian and Laird, now mum and dad, have just welcomed their little boy Hamish into the world. One week after giving birth, Valerian begins a few light workouts. She wasn't starting this post-pregnancy training from nothing – she'd been training, within her limits, up until a month before giving birth. No sparring of course.

And with Hamish now alongside them, Laird mapped out a schedule that would see Valerian competing in Australia's Gold Coast in a few months at the Commonwealth Games. Laird had searched around to see if there were case studies of other athletes who had attempted to return to top-level competition so soon after giving birth. It turns out the literature and research on this subject is sparse, meaning Laird and Valerian were often finding their way in the dark during this comeback.

On chilly London mornings, frost covering the grass, the hazy sun rising, Hamish would be rugged up and strapped onto Laird's chest, bobbling along as dad rode his bike next to mum – jogging her way back to fitness. Then it would be home for breakfast, before strength

Valerian bringing Hamish to a training session at the boxing gym in 2018

and conditioning workouts during the day. In the evenings they'd be in the gym, Valerian tinkering on the technical side of her boxing, before gradually building up to sparring – Laird in her corner every session, Hamish sleeping away in his pram next to the ring or the punching bag, mum and dad keeping close watch on their little bundle of pride and joy.

This was the routine that got her ready to compete at world level again so soon after giving birth. Crucial, too, was her diet during this comeback. She had to lose the pounds after having Hamish while building up the right amount of muscle.

One of her sparring partners during this time, Ramla Ali, also helped Valerian stick to her routine. At this point in late 2017 and early 2018, Ramla, younger than Valerian, was rising through the ranks of amateur boxing. Sparring with Valerian, therefore, offered an insight into the training regime and mindset of a more experienced international boxer. Ramla remembers the motivation she drew from these sparring sessions.

"Valerian never wanted to give up. She'd just had a baby and yet she was out there training, getting ready to compete on such a big stage in a few months. After having Hamish, she bounced back. She showed me that you don't have to listen to those negative feelings or critical inner thoughts, you just keep going. I learnt from her that you need to remember the reason you started boxing, and keep going for that reason."

Four years earlier, long before they were sparring partners, Ramla recalls another memory of Valerian. It was 2014. Ramla was living with her parents in London. She was finding her way into the sport, beginning to consider boxing as a serious career. The Commonwealth Games was on in Glasgow and she was watching the boxing on a laptop in her bedroom. She had tuned in to see Valerian's first bout of the tournament – the bout discussed in chapter one of this book when Valerian, in her first international fight, scored an upset against an established boxer ranked eighth in the world.

Ramla says: *"I remember watching the coverage in the lead up to the fight and thinking, 'Damn you're going to box an*

Olympian, that's going to be tough.' Then the fight began and I was like, 'Wow, you're making this look so easy!'"

For the up-and-coming Ramla, however, who had dreams of competing on the world stage, it was more than Valerian's boxing skills that left an impression.

"Representation is so important – you can't be what you can't see," says Ramla. "But if you see another black woman having so much success, you're like, Well, I can do that too."

Ramla's career would ultimately take a similar trajectory to Valerian's. And it was conversations that the two shared during their sparring days in the lead up to the 2018 Commonwealth Games that helped shape Ramla's continued ascent in boxing.

Like Valerian, who is British-Dominican, Ramla is also a dual national. She was born in Somalia and came to England as a child refugee. Later, when her boxing career began to take off, she had a decision to make. Would she go down the path that might see her boxing for Great Britain? Or would she go down the path that saw her representing Somalia. There were pros and cons on both sides.

Years earlier, Valerian was in a similar situation when she chose to box for Dominica.

Knowing this, Ramla and her husband Richard thought it wise to talk with Valerian and Laird about what they'd learnt along the way. Ramla talks warmly when remembering these conversations.

"When thinking about all this, we really didn't know what we were doing. Laird and Valerian were a huge help. They pointed us in the right direction so we could better understand the world of global boxing and they helped us get in contact with key people. For Richard and me, we knew we wanted to go down the Somalia route, but we needed that little bit of help from people who had done something similar already. Valerian and Laird gave us the blueprint on how to do it, which was really, really cool of them."

Valerian, Laird, Mum and Hamish (4.5 months old) at the Commonwealth Games in 2018

These discussions between the two boxing camps turned out to be a pivotal step in the progression of Ramla's career. A few years later, in 2021, she would become the first Somali boxer to compete at the Olympic Games.

When Valerian made it to Australia for the Commonwealth Games in April 2018, her first bout of the tournament did not go to plan. She didn't box well, falling short of her own expectations. Here, she couldn't help but think back to some of the reservations voiced by her dad about her comeback. This loss meant she was eliminated from the tournament. After all the work to get there, her tournament was over in 11 minutes. She was shattered.

Valerian, Mum & Hamish on the flight to the Gold Coast, Australia for the Commonwealth Games in 2018

But consider where she had come from to even get to the games and be in a position to compete, at age 38. Four months after giving birth, she had come down from 85kg, losing 28kg so she could fight in the 57kg category. She knew she wasn't anywhere near peak fitness and conditioning. But she stuck to her routine and she got there.

The Commonwealth Games in Australia hold conflicting memories for Valerian. She was proud of her efforts to get back and compete but disappointed in her performance. Her mum travelled to Australia to help look after Hamish while Valerian and Laird focused on the boxing. This support from her mum, who wasn't the biggest fan of her boxing when Valerian started, made a big difference.

This would be her last major tournament – and by then her dad had passed away. He had died the previous year when Valerian was five months pregnant with Hamish. Four years earlier, at her first big tournament at the Commonwealth Games in Glasgow, she remembers looking up to the stands and seeing her dad looking back at her, cheering and smiling. She wanted so much for him to be there again as she said farewell to the sport.

As it turned out, though, perhaps with her dad's encouragement still ringing in her ears, she couldn't stay away from the sport for long. After retiring from elite boxing, Valerian would become a trainer and coach. Through this, she has been passing on her wisdom and skills to new generations of boxers of all abilities and ages. She's breathing life into her own legacy.

Valerian with some of her trophy collection
(Credit: Jay Stewart)

Valerian's boxing achievements in numbers and titles

- 64 Fights
- Top 20 world-ranked boxer
- England Boxing National Champion, 2012 🥇
- Dominica Sportswoman of the Year, 2016 🏆
- 2 x Commonwealth Games, 2014, 2018
- 2 x World Championships, 2014, 2016
- Pan American Games, 2015
- Olympic Solidarity Scholarship holder
- America's Continental Championship, 2016, bronze 🥉
- 2 x AIBA Nations Cup International Tournament, 2015, bronze 🥉; 2016, silver 🥈
- English Title Belt Champion, 2016 🥇
- Best Senior Boxer, Islington Boxing Club, 2014 🏆
- London Captain, London Select v Denmark Select, 2016 🏆

THE BACK PAGE – VALERIAN'S AFTERWORD

I now view many of the moments and stories mentioned in the book in a new light. I was diagnosed with ADHD at the age of 43.

Really, I'd known my whole adult life, but hadn't given it much thought since I'd 'self-diagnosed' in my early 20s. I was relieved to get the official diagnosis. It explained a lot of unanswered questions from my childhood – and adult life.

The introduction talks about "my nagging feeling of drift" and "restlessness". This is something I vividly recall as a young child: if I was too still for any length of time, these feelings would come on. Now, I look back and understand my diagnosis better. I can see how sport let me channel that restlessness and energy into some sort of focus.

People are intrigued when they learn that I started boxing at 30. And, initially, I was worried about not being taken seriously as a woman in boxing. The worry stemmed from what I'd heard from the female boxers who had come before me. Plus, it still was an old school sport when I started out.

At the beginning of my career, I felt I was leading a double life. When I finished work in the office, I'd scrub my make-up off, remove my heels, put on my boxing shorts and vest and wrap around my bandana.

I rarely allowed my two worlds to come together. I carried on this double life for years. The only way in my mind to be taken seriously was to arrive at the gym looking and acting the part. I wanted to be seen as a boxer. I didn't want to be seen by others in the boxing world as a woman turning up from the office.

I became one of the most dedicated boxers in the gym and, as it turned out, I was fully welcomed, accepted and supported.

Boxing gyms can often appear as a masculine environment, and may not seem all that welcoming to women. The gym can be a dirty, sweaty community hall full of young men, and it's often a very non-politically correct place. But, once inside for any length of time, you're likely to find a friendly, community hub, with members working together to better themselves as people and boxers. The dedication I saw from the volunteer coaches in those early years, full of passion and drive, will forever remain a source of inspiration.

I did see bias against female boxers, but it usually wasn't coming from the boxing world. I heard it mostly from people I knew in my non-boxing world, once I began to reveal my double life. Some interesting questions I got were:

Why are you doing boxing, you'll get brain damage? You're too pretty to box. You must be an angry person to box.

As I began to progress, these comments from others frittered away.

I was very aware that I was always one of the oldest boxers in the gym and at any tournament. One of my first boxing coaches used to call me "The Old Boiler", which made me laugh.

He also used to say, *'If only you'd started 10 years earlier."* He was right, of course, but because I had started later in life, I had tunnel vision about what I wanted to achieve and how I needed to do it. I made the most of it and created opportunities where I could until the door firmly closed – and then change course if necessary.

I didn't have the luxury of time to develop steadily as a boxer and would sometimes accept fights before I was competently ready. I knew however that this would ultimately make me a better fighter. The flip side of this would be that I often over-think situations and imposter syndrome crept in.

Boxing places as much emphasis on the mental as it does the physical. I found I was able to control the negative self-chatter better as my mental preparations grew more automated. Routines became not just about the physical day-to-day tasks, but also about my mental preparations, keeping me focused and on track, not allowing my mind to drift towards procrastination, or get wrapped up in the minutiae of life.

After years as a boxer, thinking I was the only one with unhelpful dialogue in my head, I now see the similar patterns in many of the boxers I coach. I am grateful that I can pass on my knowledge and experience to new generations of boxers. I am honoured to be an Ambassador for Boxing Futures, part of the team that's helping improve young lives through non-contact boxing and emotional support. And I'm a proud supporter of Boxfit's Together We Box Campaign, promoting women in boxing.

And a project really close to my heart is Empower Box, a community interest company, or social enterprise. I established it in East London to help young people and adults improve their mental health and physical wellbeing through boxing and mindfulness programmes, and certifications. Now that I know what I know about my own ADHD, Empower Box has a focus on supporting girls and women with ADHD. I couldn't have started this venture without the support from Investec, an international banking and wealth management group, and the Bromley by Bow Centre, a pioneering community hub in my area of East London. Thank you.

The irony of boxing is that while it can be one of the loneliest and scariest sports in the world, it's impossible to achieve success in the sport without the support of your team and family.

My heartfelt thanks go out to my partner Laird, children, Hamish and Ceana, my mum, Helena, and my late dad Keith. Thank you to my siblings Florna and Adrian, and my boxing family – Chadwell St Mary Boxing Club,

Broad Street Boxing Club, Islington Boxing Club and the Dominican Coaches McNeil Jules and Job Joseph. Also thanks to Limehouse Boxing Academy, where I'm now an England boxing coach. Lastly, many thanks to my friend and mentor Peter Rosen. Without you all, I wouldn't have been able to do what I've done, and am doing.

Valerian, Laird, Hamish and Ceana 2025 *(Credit: Asia Giuliani)*

TESTIMONIALS

PATIENT, HUMBLE, LETHAL WEAPON

I met Valerian in late 2023. I had landed a role in a film that meant I would need to learn all about the inner workings of boxing. I was to play a boxing coach in a biopic about the life of Ramla Ali, another story of grit and finding a way against the odds.

Naturally, I needed to find a coach who I could box with, shadow, learn from and ask an endless stream of questions.

I grew up watching boxing.

If a Barry McGuigan fight was on, me and mum would settle into the living room and watch the formidable Irishman relentlessly wear down his opponent. He was as aggressive as he was precise – a difficult duo of traits to counter if you found yourself on the receiving end of a barrage from Barry.

To me, Barry was a giant: the stature of the man, the way he walked into the ring, the way he held himself while boxing. It was only later on, when I saw him standing next to other boxers in different weight categories, that I realised he was noticeably smaller than the heavyweights.

Gershwyn in training with Valerian ahead of filming In The Shadows, a biopic about the life of Ramla Ali

It was his work rate that me and mum admired the most. As others waned during a fight, Barry got more energy. No doubt his fitness was supreme, but I'm sure some of this can be put down to his mindset and his purposeful body language. Confidence, real or faked, is confidence all the same – a message I was reminded of in the pages of this book.

As soon as I walked through the door of that East London gym and met Valerian, I knew she was the right person to work with. We chatted about the role I was to play and how she might help me.

Instantly, I sensed a humility in her. Then, as we chatted more and as our sessions progressed over the next six months, I came to see a deep intelligence in her. I came to see how she tries to understand problems and people and situations from many angles. This likely explains why she was such an impressive fighter: her ability to see angles and openings where others couldn't – and then had the speed and power to act on them. Boom.

It was often on my mind that here is a woman who, if she wanted to, could transform into a lethal weapon and knock most people out in one punch. But this lethal weapon is tempered with great humility and it made her a fantastic colleague and mentor, and now friend.

I say Valerian was the right person to meet at the right time for two reasons. First, when we met I was not in great shape. I had badly injured my knee playing football about two years before I began the boxing role. When I started training with Valerian, I was unfit and my body was stiff. She was patient with me when she needed to be, and when she felt I needed to step it up, she'd encourage and expect more. I respect that.

There were moments in the ring with Valerian when she'd be explaining something to me, and I'd be like, *Oh, yeah, I can use that to do this little combination with a person.* I'd see how she creates time and space in the ring. I'm always going to bring it back to football. The great strikers are able to create time for themselves, and with boxers the great ones can create time and space to take advantage of the person in front of them, picking up on the little things a person is doing, rather than breathing heavy with arms all over the place.

With Valerian, it's like a Mr Miyagi in the ring with you. She used to get this tiny smile in the corner of her mouth when I could see she could see an opening. It's funny because she's trying to hide it, and when I started to see it, she tried to hide it more. I could see she was about ten steps ahead of me and then she could see that I could see that. It still makes me smile.

The other reason why Valerian was the right person to meet and learn from was because when we met I was going through an emotionally difficult time. On top of the injury that I was coming back from, my mum was unwell and I'd taken some time out to help care for her. Here, it was Valerian's patience I fondly recall. I knew I had to learn and improve, to make sure I did the role justice, and she knew this. Her patience and humanity towards me, while ensuring we got the job done, has left a lasting impression.

And I know she's bringing all of these traits to her post-boxing career, in the coaching gigs and social business ventures she's got up and running.

Like Valerian, who began boxing at age 30 after realising that her previous career wasn't for her, I too chose to change course. I became an actor later than most. At 25, I decided to make the full-time switch.

Found within the pages of this book are the stories and the seeds of everyday wisdom I can call on to continue listening to my dreams so I don't die with the music in me.

Thank you, Valerian for welcoming me into your gym and into your world, and thank you for being so generous in letting me into your boxing brain. Thank you, too, to Laird and your wonderful kids who welcomed me with open arms. The family focus of the boxing world you showed me was truly special.

Through hard work and focus, Valerian saw the fruits of her labour. And as much as her achievements are remarkable, the type of person she is an even bigger achievement.

This is one of the many gems of a lesson I have drawn from reading Valerian's story. It's a timely book for me – relatable, readable, with bite-sized lessons that I believe lots of people might apply to many aspects of their lives and careers. I know I will.

Gershwyn Eustache Jnr,
Actor

Round by Round tells the story of a woman who, at 30 years of age, undertook a remarkable journey in boxing. With self-belief in her corner, in only a few years she graduated from novice to champion!

Valerian Spicer describes her journey, and above all, the methods, and disciplines she conceived of to provide her with focus, to get fit, overcome setbacks, and ultimately, to achieve championship success in her chosen sport.

Thanks to reading of the 'Spicer Method', we can also learn how to achieve and become more purposeful and fulfilled, whatever challenges we face in our own lives.

Callum Morrison, Head of Entrepreneurship,
Coventry University